I0074649

The Gold, Sliver, and Hourglass Standard

A discussion about the Origins of Money

ANOTHER GOOD DAY WITH GOD

ANOTHER GOOD DAY WITH GOD

Title:
The Gold, Sliver, and
Hourglass Standard.

Copyright © 2017, **1st Edition**

Author: J.Jordan

ANOTHER GOOD DAY WITH GOD,
PUBLISHING

Messages to the Publisher/Author
of this Book can be posted at:

LastChancePetition.com
CaptainPetition.com

ISBN 10: 0-9916107-0-9
ISBN 13: 978-0-9916107-0-9

ANOTHER GOOD DAY WITH GOD

I Give Thanks to
My Very Good Friend

GOD

**the Creator of
the Universe**
Who Inspired Me to
Complete this Book

ANOTHER GOOD DAY WITH GOD

======================================

TABLE OF CONTENTS

======================================

ANOTHER GOOD DAY WITH GOD

ANOTHER GOOD DAY WITH GOD

ANOTHER GOOD DAY WITH GOD

T

ANOTHER GOOD DAY WITH
GOD

ANOTHER GOOD DAY WITH GOD

An attempt was done to arrange the Chapters in a sequence that is relevant to the details discussed, however, the Chapters of this book are not necessarily meant to be reviewed in any particular order, and each Chapter could be construed as being a separate discussion in and of itself.

The Chapters in this book are not necessarily complete, and have been put into this book for your immediate review.

One of the main purposes of this book is to describe what real money is and the value of real money to allow the domestic and international Public Markets to immediately begin Using and Storing real money, in addition to, or instead of, only Using and Storing the risky paper money that is not pegged to anything with an alleged value such as gold and silver.

ANOTHER GOOD DAY WITH GOD

ANOTHER GOOD DAY WITH GOD

```
====================================
WHAT IS MONEY ?                    2
====================================
```

Every "country" with "money", has
a history of money, and therefore,
one way to get a description of
"money" is to review "the history
of money" for the previous 1000
years, such as the history of
roman coins.

In simple terms, "money" is a
tangible "item" that is used as a
BARTER "item"; presumably, any
tangible "item" can be used as
"money" during a two-way BARTER
transaction; paper "money" is also
a BARTER "item";

Some simple examples of "money"
are:

* SHOES
* PIECES OF METAL
* WHEAT GRAIN
* HEMP SEED
* CLOTHE
* HOUSES
* TABLES & CHAIRS
* et cetera

ANOTHER GOOD DAY WITH GOD

Using one "item" to "pay for" a different "item", is another way of saying... using one "item" to BARTER for a different "item", such as...

(1) a COIN is an item, that can be used to BARTER for another item, such as a LOAF OF BREAD.

(2) a PAIR OF SHOES is an "item", that can be used to BARTER for another "item", such as a COIN.

(3) a CHAIR is an "item", that can be used to BARTER for another "item",
such as a PAIR OF SHOES.

(4) a HOUSE is an "item", that can be used to BARTER for other "items", such as a different HOUSE and some COINS.

(5) a PIECE OF PAPER MONEY is an "item", that can be used to BARTER for other "items", such as a HOUSE and some COINS.

16

ANOTHER GOOD DAY WITH GOD

Obviously, there is an entire list of BARTER items that can be used as "money" in a public market, and each BARTER item has a unique characteristic pertaining to:

* SIZE
* WEIGHT
* DIVISIBILITY
* SHELF-LIFE
* APPEARANCE
* QUALITY
* SUPPLY
* DEMAND
* RISK INVOLVED
* ET CETERA

For example, a COIN would have a size, weight, shelf-life, appearance, quality, and a supply & demand.

And a sack of grain would have a size, weight, shelf-life, appearance, quality, and a supply & demand.

And a pair of shoes would have a size, weight, shelf-life, appearance, quality, and a supply & demand.

ANOTHER GOOD DAY WITH GOD

Throughout the years, because of the various characteristics of each BARTER item, some BARTER items (apparently) became more accepted and used as "money" than other BARTER items within the Public Markets.

Many of the early forms of money are very simple, effective, and fair.

Many of those early forms of money can still be easily used today in all domestic and foreign markets.

ANOTHER GOOD DAY WITH GOD

3

What is "tender", and what is "legal tender" ?

"Tender" is just another way of saying: "Money", and,

"Legal Tender" is just another way of saying: "Money that will not be taxed during a BARTER transaction" -and- "the only Money that can be used for BARTER transactions with the usa government";

Generally speaking, the usa "government" is a store in the public market, and LEGAL TENDER is the only BARTER items that the usa "government" will accept during BARTER transactions.

What BARTER items can be used as "Legal Tender" is often set by a usa "governmental" law.

ANOTHER GOOD DAY WITH GOD

For the purposes of discussing LEGAL TENDER, BARTER items can be separated into two categories:

(1) "money/barter-items" that are used as LEGAL TENDER;
(2) "money/barter-items" that are not used as legal tender.

Unless prohibited by Law, the Public Market is LEGALLY allowed to use any BARTER item during any BARTER transaction, and the Pubic Market can refrain from using LEGAL TENDER during any BARTER transaction.

BARTER transactions of goods and services not using LEGAL TENDER is often called DIRECT-TRADING.

Unless prohibited by Law, the Public Market CAN do all their barter transactions using all types of BARTER items (e.g. COMMON TENDER, such as grain, cotton, silver), that may or may not include some LEGAL TENDER as one of the BARTER items.

ANOTHER GOOD DAY WITH GOD

An example of when the Public Market is legally required to use LEGAL TENDER during a BARTER trade is when trading with the usa "government" itself, such as:

3

(1) giving "money" (e.g. taxes) to the usa "government" in exchange for their "services", or,

(2) getting "money" (e.g. getting a paycheck) from the usa "government".

Designating a certain BARTER item as LEGAL TENDER is more convenient for the usa "government" to BARTER with the "residents".

ANOTHER GOOD DAY WITH GOD

ANOTHER GOOD DAY WITH GOD

What is the value of a sack of
grain ?

What is the value of a pair of new
shoes ?

What is the value of a silver
bar ?

Can you describe the barter values
of grain, shoes, and silver, in
relation to each other ?

How can buyers and sellers in the
domestic and international public
markets get a fair barter trade if
they can not describe the values
of common items such as grain,
shoes, and silver ?

For example, how much grain should you trade for a pair of shoes or a silver bar, during a BARTER transaction ?

If you can not answer those simple questions, then perhaps you need to IGNORE the money changers and _their_ mainstream economics, and continue reviewing this book and the "hourglass standard" as presented in this book for a better ability to compare the BARTER value of all BARTER items.

As previously said, Money is an "item", such as a pair of shoes, or a sack of grain;

Money, as an "item", can also be called a TOKEN; for example, some people call various small "items" TOKENS, such as unmarked coins or similar trinkets.

As such, all BARTER "items" can be called TOKENS; for example, grain, shoes, houses, silver, coins, etc, can all be called TOKENS.

ANOTHER GOOD DAY WITH GOD

Traditionally, the real value of any TOKEN was largely based on the **labor-time needed to produce the TOKEN**,

For example, a person baking a loaf of bread will produce an edible TOKEN OF TIME, and the value of the loaf of bread has the same exact value as the labor-time that was needed to produce the loaf of bread;

The loaf of bread is an edible TOKEN OF TIME that can can be BARTERED for other TOKENS OF TIME in the public market, or the TOKEN OF TIME can be used to BARTER with someone for their labor-time.

And therefore, each BARTER "item" during a BARTER transaction can be called a TOKEN OF TIME that has the same exact value as the labor-time needed to produce the TOKEN OF TIME;

Hence BARTER "items" can be called TOKENS OF TIME.

ANOTHER GOOD DAY WITH GOD

Generally speaking, early money, such as the early Roman and Greek coins, were also TOKENS OF TIME that were used to BARTER for other TOKENS OF TIME, such as a loaf of bread;

Each of those non-edible coined TOKENS OF TIME each had a weight of metal, and the value of each of those TOKENS OF TIME was equivalent to the labor-time involved in getting/producing that weight of metal;

Traditionally, the BARTER value of any "item" presented during a BARTER transaction was often determined by the LABOR-TIME involved in getting/producing that "item".

ANOTHER GOOD DAY WITH GOD

5

One conclusion of this book is to explain about using the "hourglass standard" to determine the value of BARTER items, instead of arbitrarily using a "gold standard", or a "silver standard", et cetera, to determine the value of BARTER items;

The "hourglass standard" is simple and just determines the amount of TIME is involved in any particular "TOKEN OF TIME".

After obtaining the average xyz amount of time that is needed to produce and item or service, then that xyz amount of time can be used to set the value of the item; items can then be bartered in the public market based on the xyz amount of time needed to produce the "parts & labor" of the items being bartered.

ANOTHER GOOD DAY WITH GOD

For example, if 1 hour "parts & labor" is needed to produce a 100 gram sack of grain, and 2 hours "parts & labor" is needed to produce a pair of shoes, and 9 hours "parts & labor" is needed to produce 1 gram of silver, then:

1 hour = 1 sack of grain
2 hours = 1 pair of shoes
9 hours = 100 grams silver

The 2 hour price of 2 sacks of grain has the same 2 hour price as 1 pair of shoes;

The 9 hour price of 100 grams of silver has the same 9 hour price as 9 sacks of grain;

The 9 hour price of 100 grams of silver also has the same 9 hour price as 4 pairs of shoes with an hourglass of silver remaining (11 grams) that could be used to trade for a sack of grain; Et Cetera.

ANOTHER GOOD DAY WITH GOD

For the purposes of determining the value of items for bartering purposes, what column below has similar items that can be easily compared?

5

ANOTHER GOOD DAY WITH GOD

ANOTHER GOOD DAY WITH GOD

```
=====================================
GOLD, SILVER, AND
ET CETERA STANDARDS              6
=====================================
```

What is a gold standard ?

What is a silver standard ?

What is a "money" standard ?

Who needs those standards, and who sets those standards ?

Often, a monetary standard is just a declared standard that sets an arbitrary number to a certain quantity of a particular item, such as saying that 1 gram of gold or silver will have the arbitrary number 1 and then stamping the 1 on the metal or printed on a piece of paper.

A monetary standard can be set by a law, or can be set by the public market.

ANOTHER GOOD DAY WITH GOD

If a standard such as a gold standard is set by a usa "government" law, then it is the usa "government" who sets the gold standard, and the same can be said for any other standard, such as a silver standard.

Although, the public market could also set a "gold standard", when has anyone heard of the public market setting a "gold standard", or any other "standard", in relation to paper money ?

The public market does not need to wait for the usa "government" to set a "gold standard", "silver standard", "et cetera standard", and can do barter transactions without those usa "government" standards.

ANOTHER GOOD DAY WITH GOD

Perhaps much of the hype about wanting the usa "government" to set a "gold standard", "silver standard", et cetera, is coming from persons who own and are hoarding a bulk of the gold and silver, who are wanting the usa "government" to set a law that forces a value increase of their gold and silver.

Actually, the usa "government" already has a "gold standard" and a "silver standard" if the usa "government" sells gold coins and silver coins; the "gold standard" or "silver standard" is simply set by the amount of gold coins and silver coins that the usa "government" will exchange for paper money.

As discussed in a previous chapter, using the hourglass standard is perhaps a more fair method of determining the price of many goods and services, rather than using a "gold standard", or a "silver standard";

ANOTHER GOOD DAY WITH GOD

Apart from "supply & demand", many ancient goods and services, such as in ancient Rome and Greece, probably all were valued using the hourglass standard.

ANOTHER GOOD DAY WITH GOD

==================================
WHAT IS THE "DENOMINATION" OF
MONEY; AND A PRESENT NEED FOR
"COMPARISON CHARTS" TO COMPARE THE
"HOURGLASS STANDARD" TO BARTER
ITEMS;   7
==================================

The use of "denominations" to
"denominate" the value of money
can, and probably has been,
manipulated throughout the
decades.

Originally, metal money and many
other BARTER items, probably were
"denominated" by weight, such as 1
gram, or 1 kilogram;

After many years of using those
"denominations of weight" in the
Public Market, those
"denominations of weight" probably
just became an arbitrary
"denominations" in the Public
Market, such as a piece of metal
that was previously hand stamped
as "1 gram", later began to be
hand stamped with just the "1"
stamped on the metal;

ANOTHER GOOD DAY WITH GOD

After years of using the arbitrary "1" on the pieces of metal, the Public Market just began referring to the pieces of metal as 1's, 2's, 5's, etc;

Also, the arbitrary "1" was also used when BARTERING other BARTER items, such as a Pair of Shoes was BARTERED for 100 pieces of metal, rather than "100 grams" of metal;

Most of the Public Market began to disassociate any weight to the pieces of metal and other BARTER items;

Because no weight was associated with the value of "1", the usa "government" was able to decrease the weight of the pieces of metal that had began to be used as "money", while continuing to hand stamping the "1" on the pieces of metal;

ANOTHER GOOD DAY WITH GOD

Most of the Public Market did not complain about the devalued weight because most of the Public Market was no longer familiar with the origins of the "1" and therefore, the Public Market did not associate the "1" with "1 gram";

Throughout the years of use, the denomination of "1 gram" could be changed to an arbitrary "1", and then changed to "1 cent";

Similar to the "1", the weight of "100 grams" could be changed to "100", and then later changed to "1 dollar";

As a result of the Public Market not using "denominations of weight" to determine the sale price of metal and other BARTER items, the Public Market began to accept devalued money.

After the habitual use of arbitrary units of "money", such as "1 cent" and "1 dollar", the Public Market has stopped using "denominations of weight", such as "1 gram" and "1 kilogram";

7

ANOTHER GOOD DAY WITH GOD

The Public Market of today, could begin to use "denominations of weight" again, and begin to use the "hourglass standard", when pricing goods and services in the Public Market, however, there may be hesitation to use other "denominations" until someone publishes a comparison chart that compares the XYZ amount of time that is needed to produce any particular good or service offered in the Public Market;

For example, XYZ amount of time is needed to produce "100 grams" of metal, and XYZ amount of time is needed to produce a pair of shoes, and therefore, if 10 hours is needed to produce "100 grams" of metal, and 2 hours is needed to produce a pair of shoes, then the pair of shoes has the same value as 20 grams of metal "money";

ANOTHER GOOD DAY WITH GOD

After the comparison chart is published and distributed to the Public Markets, then the Buyers and Sellers in the Public Markets can easily use the Comparison Chart to accept many more BARTER items as "money" instead of being limited to "legal tender".

7

ANOTHER GOOD DAY WITH GOD

AN EXAMPLE OF A COMPARISON CHART:

1 HOUR OF SEMI-SKILLED LABOR CAN PRODUCE 5 POUNDS OF WHEAT GRAIN.

1 HOUR OF SEMI-SKILLED LABOR CAN PRODUCE 4 POUNDS OF CORN GRAIN.

1 HOUR OF SEMI-SKILLED LABOR CAN PRODUCE 7 POUNDS OF HEMP SEED.

4 HOURS OF SEMI-SKILLED LABOR CAN PRODUCE 1 PAIR OF SHOES.

1 HOUR OF SEMI-SKILLED LABOR CAN PRODUCE 1 GRAM SILVER.

LABOR REQUIRED	=	PRODUCT
1 HOUR		1 POUNDS WHEAT GRAIN
1 HOUR		1 POUNDS OF CORN GRAIN
1 HOUR		1 POUNDS OF HEMP SEED
4 HOURS		1 PAIR AVERAGE SHOES
1-100 HOURS		1 GRAM SILVER

ANOTHER GOOD DAY WITH GOD

THE PREVIOUS COMPARISON CHART DOES
NOT INCLUDE THE
SUPPLY/DEMAND/EXPERIENCE-OF-LABOR
FACTORS;

FOR EXAMPLE, A DENTIST CAN DO 1
HOUR OF LABOR, BUT REQUIRES MANY
MONTHS EXPERIENCE, AND CAN
THEREFORE A DENTIST CAN ASK THE
BUYER FOR 20 HOURS OF GRAIN IN
EXCHANGE FOR 1 HOUR OF LABOR;

7

THERE IS A SUPPLY/DEMAND FACTOR
ALSO, AND THERE MAY BE 40 DENTISTS
IN TOWN, AND THE BUYER MAY AGREE
TO PAY 15 HOURS OF GRAIN.

ANOTHER GOOD DAY WITH GOD

USING THE PREVIOUS COMPARISON
CHART, 20 POUNDS OF GRAIN HAS THE
SAME VALUE AS 1 PAIR OF SHOES; A
VENDOR IN THE PUBLIC MARKET CAN
EASILY REVIEW THE COMPARISON
CHART, AND THEN INCLUDE MORE
PRICES INTO THEIR PRICE TAGS, SUCH
AS SELLING 1 PAIR OF SHOES USING A
PRICE LABEL THAT INCLUDES ALL OF
THE FOLLOWING...

            - PRICE TAG -
          1 PAIR OF SHOES

 Money that will be Accepted:
 (a) $20 legal tender
 (b) 1 gram Silver
 (c) 7 kilograms Hemp Seed
 [Et Cetera]

ANOTHER GOOD DAY WITH GOD

Several hundred years ago, there were a limited amount of items being produced for the "Public Market", and it seems that many of those same items produced for "sale", were also used as "money", such as sacks of Grain and Salt;

7

Because of the very limited amount of items that were produced hundreds of years ago, such "Comparison Charts" as described in this Chapter were already familiar by most everyone in the Public Markets;

For example, just about everyone in town was familiar with what everyone else in town was doing for work, and just about everyone in town was familiar with how much time/labor was needed to produce any particular item; aside from the supply/demand and the issues with "experienced labor", just about everyone in the Public Market wanted a fair 1-to-1 exchange of goods and services, and no one in the Public Market could easily be swindled by another Buyer or Seller;

ANOTHER GOOD DAY WITH GOD

For example, Traders in the Public Market presumably would trade 1 hour of hemp seed for 1 hour of corn grain, but I could not be swindled to trade 2 hours of hemp seed for 1 hour of corn grain;

Today, there are hundreds of goods in the Public Market that could be used as "money", however, the Public Market does not seem to have a readily available "Comparison Chart" to compare the Hourglass value of items that are being traded;

The lack of a "Comparison Chart" presumably is the result of the Public Market using arbitrary denominations such as "1 cent" and "1 dollar", instead of trading using "denominations of weight" such as "1 gram" and "1 kilogram", that would have been further based on "denomination of time (labor)";

ANOTHER GOOD DAY WITH GOD

Using the "hourglass standard" inside a Comparison Chart will allow the domestic and international Public Markets to accept more forms of "money" as payment;

Also, using a Comparison Chart will hinder swindlers from overprinting paper money and devaluing metal-based money.

7

When arbitrary denominations on "money" are used, the Public Markets seems to easily accepting devalued "money" when the weight of the "money" is reduced.

ANOTHER GOOD DAY WITH GOD

"Denominations of Weight" have been used for centuries, and if the Public Markets today once again begin using "Denominations of Weight", such as "1 gram" instead of "1 cent", along with a Comparison Chart that compares those "denominations of weights" to the "denominations of time (labor)" needed to produce that type of "money", along with a comparison to the various other goods and services in the Public Markets, then the Buyers and Sellers will once again be able to use traditional "money" in the domestic and international Public Markets.

The ability of the Public Market to transition to accepting various common BARTER items as "money" in the Public Markets can be easily implemented just by providing the Public Market with a Comparison Chart, along with telling all the Sellers in the Public Market that they can easily accept other "forms of payment" on their "price tags".

ANOTHER GOOD DAY WITH GOD

It seems that drastic changes to
any "current monetary system"
would not need to be done, because
many different BARTER items can be
used as "money" at the same time
that "legal tender" is used as
"money";

The Buyers and Sellers can decide
themselves what they Buyers and
Sellers want to use as "money"
during any particular BARTER
transaction;

For example, a Buyer can offer the
Seller some "legal tender" in
exchange for a Pair of Shoes, and
the Seller can tell the Buyer that
the Buyer needs to go exchange
their "paper money" for 2 pounds
of hemp seed somewhere and then
return to do the BARTER
transaction;

When implementing the "hourglass
standard", the "paper money" does
not need to be immediately
canceled by the usa "government";

ANOTHER GOOD DAY WITH GOD

If desired, the usa "government" can also begin to accept certain other common BARTER items as "taxes", in addition to the "paper money".

If the Public Market begins commonly accepting other BARTER items as "money", then it allows the Public Market to eventually refuse "paper money".

The Buyers and Sellers in the Public Market are the only persons hindering competing currencies at the cash register, not the "government" or the "central banks".

Determining the actual prices of "goods and services" at the cash register can perhaps be more easily done, after various independent evaluations are done using a Comparison Chart, to put a "hourglass price tag" on the various "goods and services" using the hourglass standard;

ANOTHER GOOD DAY WITH GOD

The purpose of the independent Comparison Charts is just to compare the common and average hourglass prices of goods and services; and the Public Market does not need to accept just one independent Comparison Chart; there can be several independent Comparison Charts all done at the same time, such as a dozen Comparison Charts done across several countries; eventually, a couple independent Comparison Charts will be accepted in the domestic and international Public Markets for use during BARTER transactions.

7

Determining the hourglass prices of goods and services will need to Compare the amount of time that is needed to produce all the different goods and services in the Comparison Chart, such as the amount of hourglass time needed for labor, and the amount of hourglass time that was needed for the materials needed to produce an item.

ANOTHER GOOD DAY WITH GOD

Also, determining the hourglass price for an item may also need to set an average hourglass time, somewhere between the amount of hourglass time needed to produce the item using machine labor and manual labor...

For example:

LABOR REQUIRED	=	PRODUCT PRODUCED
14 HOURS manual labor		1000 kg HEMP SEED, dry
1 HOUR machine labor		1000 kg HEMP SEED, dry
2 HOURS suggested average		1000 kg HEMP SEED, dry

In the above example, 1 hourglass of machine labor is needed to produce 1000 kg Hemp Seed, however, the average price for both machine labor and manual labor could be set to 2 hourglasses to set the average, and to pay for the machine;

For example:

It costs hourglasses to produce a machine...

LABOR REQUIRED	=	PRODUCT PRODUCED
3120 HOURS		Machine to collect and process Hemp Seed, with expected 70,000 hours of machine life (20 years)

7

If accurate time cards are kept, it can be determined that a Hemp Seed machine needs 3120 Hours to be produced, and it can then be determined that the Hemp Seed machine can produce 70,000 hours of Hemp Seed, and therefore, 3120 hours labor / 70,000 hours use = 0.045 hours that could be included with the 1 hourglass value for 1000 kg of Hemp Seed resulting in a sale price of about 1.045 hourglasses for 1000 kg of Hemp Seed produced with a Hemp Seed machine;

ANOTHER GOOD DAY WITH GOD

However, determining the final hourglass price to produce and use the Hemp Seed machine will also need to account for the hourglass prices of all the items that are needed to produce and use the machine...

For example:

LABOR REQUIRED	=	PRODUCT PRODUCED
20 HOURS		1 Tire
20 HOURS		Raw Rubber for 1 Tire, 1000 kg
1 HOURS		1 liter fuel
40 HOURS		20 years routine maintenance

ANOTHER GOOD DAY WITH GOD

And as for other Goods & Services, there may be a need for a certain method to determine the hourglass price of certain Services...

For example:

LABOR REQUIRED	=	PRODUCT PRODUCED
7000 HOURS		(2 years) Dentist Training
25000 HOURS		Trainee pays 25000 hourglasses of Hemp Seed or other product for the Dentist Training
1 HOUR		1 hour Dental work
2 HOURS suggested average		1 hour Dental work

The above Comparison Chart table indicates that the Dentist can charge 2 hourglasses for 1 hourglass work, at least until the other items are paid.

And there are other examples...

LABOR REQUIRED	=	PRODUCT PRODUCED
14000 HOURS		(4 years) Lawyer Training
70000 HOURS		Trainee pays 70000 hourglasses of Hemp Seed or other product for the Lawyer Training
1 HOUR		1 hour Lawyer work
2 HOUR suggested average		1 hour Lawyer work

LABOR REQUIRED	=	PRODUCT PRODUCED
1 HOUR		Dishwasher Training
0 HOURS		Trainee pays 0 hourglasses of product for the Dishwasher Training
1 HOUR		1 hour Dishwasher work

ANOTHER GOOD DAY WITH GOD

LABOR REQUIRED	=	PRODUCT PRODUCED
14000 HOURS		(4 years) total Mechanic TRAINING/EXPERIENCE
2 HOURS		Mechanic TRAINING to change a Tire
1 HOUR		1 hour Mechanic LABOR needed to change a Tire
20 HOURS		Mechanic TRAINING to adjust engine timing
1 HOUR		1 hour Mechanic LABOR to adjust engine timing
? HOURS average		? Product Above

Using the above Comparison Charts, 1 hourglasses of 1 liters fuel could be exchanged evenly for 1 hour LABOR to adjust engine timing;

ANOTHER GOOD DAY WITH GOD

If the products being traded each requires significant experience/training, then the extra experience/training could also be included in the price for both the products being traded;

For example, 1 hourglass of fuel could perhaps be exchanged fairly for 1.1 hourglass of LABOR to wash dishes at a restaurant because not very much training is needed to wash dishes;

Whereas 1 hourglass of fuel could perhaps be exchanged evenly for the 1 hourglass LABOR to adjust the engine timing because a certain amount of experience is needed to produce 1 hourglass of fuel, and a certain amount of experience is needed to adjust the engine timing;

ANOTHER GOOD DAY WITH GOD

Of course, the Comparison Chart for Labor that shows the Experience/Training required for a task can also be used for setting base prices for bartering purposes, however, without Laws setting prices, certain professions such as Lawyers may want to set their prices to receive extreme profits.

7

Also, the Comparison Chart may just want to show the actual hourglass prices to print and bind certain items such as books and magazines, and then explain that the author can charge whatever the author wants.

In conclusion, to form a good Comparison Chart, the xyz amount of LABOR needed to produce an item needs to be documented, and the xyz amount of EXPERIENCE/TRAINING may also need to be documented;

ANOTHER GOOD DAY WITH GOD

It may be important to note, that some of the Tables above began this discussion using the end products, such as 1000kg hemp seed, and then continued the discussion to another product, such as the hemp seed machine, and then the other products such as the tires;

However, while producing a Comparison Chart for products, it may be better to begin the hourglass evaluations from the first stage raw materials, and then continue the Comparison Chart to the end products.

Also, to get certain products into the comparison charts first for "money" purposes, it may be better to evaluate items such as silver, copper, stainless steel, nickel, aluminum, gold, et cetera, to establish their "hourglass" standards according to their weights and processes, such as 10 hours labor produces 1 gram silver with process A, and 15 hours labor produces 1 gram silver with process B.

ANOTHER GOOD DAY WITH GOD

```
===================================
17,000 YEARS OF
THE HOURGLASS STANDARD IN USE     8
===================================
```

[A STORY OF MONEY IN A SMALL
TOWN, 17000 YEARS AGO]

In this example, the hourglass **8**
standard is in daily use will be
discussed.

About 17000 years ago, there was a
fictional town with an average
population of 27.

Throughout the years, the 27
residents of this town were able
to produce wheat, bread, clothes,
shoes, and copper, and also were
skilled in metrology - the study
of weights and measurements.

ANOTHER GOOD DAY WITH GOD

[THE TOWN, AFTER HUNDREDS OF YEARS WHEAT PRODUCTION]

During the following several hundred years, many of the residents were still producing the grain for food and seed, and had various tasks to do to produce that grain; for example, after cutting the wheat stalks, the wheat was gathered and dried; the wheat was then pounded to separate the grains from the stalks; some grain was eaten; some grain was used as seed; on Sundays, those persons rested, and on the other days of the week, those persons did their labor, six days a week, week after week, month after month, year after year, for hundreds of years.

After sowing and harvesting wheat for hundreds of years, do you believe that the residents sowing and harvesting the wheat grain would be able to describe the AVERAGE xyz amount of time that was needed to produce 100 grams of wheat grain ?

ANOTHER GOOD DAY WITH GOD

Since this town had an average population of 27, and because this town only produced wheat, bread, clothes, shoes, and copper, do you believe that EVERY resident in that town would be able to describe the AVERAGE xyz amount of time that was needed to produce 100 grams of wheat grain ?

8

[THE BREAD, CLOTHES, SHOES, COPPER]

When the residents were not doing chores producing the wheat, many of the residents in that small town would also produce other items, such as the bread, clothes, shoes, and copper; those residents rested on Sundays and did all their labor on the other days of the week, week after week, month after month, year after year, for hundreds of years.

ANOTHER GOOD DAY WITH GOD

After doing labor for a limited amount of items for hundreds of years, do you believe that EACH residents in that town would be able to describe the AVERAGE xyz amount of time that was needed to produce 100 grams of grain, a loaf of bread, an item of clothing, a pair of shoes, or 100 grams of copper ?

If the AVERAGE xyz amount of time that was needed to produce 100 grams of grain was 1 hourglass of time, do you believe that EACH resident in that town would be able to be swindled by any visitor from a nearby town who said that 20 hourglasses of time was needed to produce 100 grams of grain ?

ANOTHER GOOD DAY WITH GOD

Within the small town, there were not very many items produced; the town was small, and every shop was within 7 miles; often, residents would socialize with other residents in that small town; all the residents were familiar with ALL of the various items produced in that small town, and all the residents in that small town were familiar with the AVERAGE xyz amount of hourglass time that was needed to produce any particular item at any particular stage of production.

Barter was not necessary within that small town, because all the residents produced their own goods, or shared the work, however, all the residents in that small town were all familiar with all the jobs being done within that small town, and were also familiar with the jobs being done in neighboring towns, and therefore, all the residents were familiar with the AVERAGE xyz amount of hourglass time that was needed to produce any particular item.

ANOTHER GOOD DAY WITH GOD

Occasionally, throughout the years, barter was done within the town and with neighboring domestic and foreign towns.

Because the residents of most domestic and foreign towns were already familiar with the AVERAGE xyz amount of hourglass time that was needed to produce any particular item, all the items bartered were direct-exchange trades unless there was a large supply & demand for an item;

For example, if someone wanted grain with a value of 1 hourglass of time, and they had a pair of shoes with a value of 2 hourglasses of time, then that person probably would just trade the pair of shoes for 2 hourglasses of grain;

ANOTHER GOOD DAY WITH GOD

If the person with the grain went to any domestic or foreign town and said they wanted 4 pairs of shoes, with a value of 8 hourglasses of time, in exchange for 1 hourglass of grain, then the person with the shoes probably would say "I'LL LITERALLY JUST PRODUCE THE GRAIN MYSELF, OR LOCATE A DIFFERENT PERSON WITH GRAIN".

8

[THE TOWN AFTER 700 YEARS]

After several hundred years, the town began rampantly OVER-BREEDING, and soon the town had a population of 27 million residents.

The natural land was decimated and polluted by much rampant OVER-BREEDING.

Because the town had a larger population, each of the residents of the town were able to narrow their jobs to producing only one or two of the 5 items produced from the wheat, bread, clothes, shoes, and copper.

ANOTHER GOOD DAY WITH GOD

Barter became more common, however, all the residents were all familiar with the AVERAGE xyz amount of time that was needed to produce any particular item in the town.

Unless there was a large supply & demand for an item, residents in the town were still saying "I'LL LITERALLY JUST PRODUCE THE GRAIN MYSELF, OR LOCATE A DIFFERENT PERSON WITH GRAIN", if someone wanted to exchange 1 hourglass of grain for 4 pairs of shoes.

[THE TOWN AFTER ANOTHER 1700 YEARS]

After several hundred more years, the town was still rampantly OVER-BREEDING, and soon the town had a population of 127 million residents.

The natural land was decimated and polluted more by all the rampant OVER-BREEDING.

ANOTHER GOOD DAY WITH GOD

Because the town had a larger
population, each residents of the
town were able to continue
producing only one or two items
produced from the wheat, bread,
clothes, shoes, and copper.

The town was still using the
hourglass standard during barter
exchanges, and the residents had a
need for all the items being
bartered; some of the items had a
good SHELF-LIFE and was divisible,
such as grain, and other items had
a really really good SHELF-LIFE
and was also divisible, such a
copper.

Many of the residents tended to
have more copper on their shelves,
because of the really really good
SHELF-LIFE, and because there
consistently was a need for copper
in the public market.

ANOTHER GOOD DAY WITH GOD

Whenever demand for copper cookware and other copper items decreased, more copper ingots were able to be BANKED on the shelves and SAVED until needed for BARTER exchanges or copper items.

Each ingot of copper maintained a ratio consisting of the AVERAGE 4 hourglasses of time that was needed to produce 200 grams of copper;

As such, each 200 grams of copper was stamped with "4 hourglasses - 200 grams"; after many years, each ingot was just stamped with "4 hourglasses", yet each resident still familiar with 4 hourglasses of copper equaling 200 grams of copper, so no one needed to complain;

After many more years, each ingot was just stamped with a larger size "4" to represent 4 hourglasses, yet each resident still familiar with 4 hourglasses of copper equaling 200 grams of copper, so no one needed to complain;

ANOTHER GOOD DAY WITH GOD

[THE TOWN AFTER ANOTHER 2700 YEARS]

After several hundred more years, the town was still rampantly OVER-BREEDING, and soon the town had a population of 1427 million residents.

8

The natural land was decimated and polluted more by all the rampant OVER-BREEDING.

Because the town had a larger population, each residents of the town were able to continue producing only one or two items produced from the wheat, bread, clothes, shoes, and copper; the town had also began producing many other items in the town;

The town also had began to mainly do their barter exchanges using the copper ingots on one side of the exchange; because the ingots were stamped with a "4" without any mention of the hourglass standard, residents just began to call the copper ingots "4 dollars";

ANOTHER GOOD DAY WITH GOD

Also, because of the dozens of items now produced in the town, each of the residents each began specializing in producing 1 or 2 items instead of all of their own items, and therefore, most of the residents became more and more unfamiliar with the AVERAGE xyz amount of hourglass time that was needed to produce any particular item that was produced by the other residents;

After residents began putting price tags on items, such as wanting "20 dollars" for 1 pair of shoes, many residents could not say what the AVERAGE amount of xyz hourglass time that "20 dollars" represented, and therefore residents could not determine what the fair barter trade is when exchanging "dollars" for a pair of shoes;

ANOTHER GOOD DAY WITH GOD

About this time, a group of
residents began to call themselves
the "government" and began a
system for getting free money
called "taxes", for their
"services"; the so-called
"government" began "regulating"
the "money"; about this time, many
of the residents and the
"government" began calling the
copper that was used during barter
transactions "coins", and about
this time the money changers began
residing in the town;

8

Because the "government" were
greedy swindlers, and also because
the "government" enjoyed getting
into wars of conquest and plunder,
the "government" wanted more
"money" to pay themselves and to
pay the "soldiers";

Whenever "coins" became scarce,
the money changers suggested to
the "government" that the
"government" could decreased the
size of the "coins" while keeping
the same number "4" on the coins;

ANOTHER GOOD DAY WITH GOD

By decreasing the weight of the coins and keeping the same generic denominations, the "government" was able to increase the money on their "BANK of shelves", and was also able to pay themselves and the "soldiers" without drastically increasing the taxes;

The money changers were involved in the "government", and therefore, the "government" allowed the money changers to debase their "coins" at the "government" "mint".

ANOTHER GOOD DAY WITH GOD

```
===================================
WHAT IS A BANK ?                  9
===================================
```

What is a bank ?

A bank is just a "public storage facility", in the simplest terms.

What are some other common "pubic storage facilities" ?

A public storage facility for storing household goods is an example of a "public storage".

An rv storage facility is another "public storage".

A grocery store is a "private storage".

A simple bank is just a "public storage" for storing LEGAL TENDER and sometimes other BARTER items such as metal bullion, and personal items that can be put into "safety deposit boxes".

ANOTHER GOOD DAY WITH GOD

Many banks seem to offer a list of services, and will therefore need to comply with many Laws and Regulations pertaining to banking transactions.

However, it is presumed that **A VERY SIMPLE BANK** that only offers the service of **STORING** "money", probably would not need to comply with very many laws;

A similar comparison to **STORING** money would be a **STORAGE FACILITY** that stored household goods, because a STORAGE FACILITY probably does not need to comply with very many laws for the service of STORING "household goods".

It is when a bank offers more services, that a bank needs to comply with more laws and regulations, such as when a bank offers various types of loans and money speculation services.

ANOTHER GOOD DAY WITH GOD

Often, many economists and others complain about the corrupt jewish central banks and their unpegged paper money, yet those same economists never discuss that all the whiners could run their own simple bank that only offers a few simple services that they were saying that all banks should be limited to.

9

Presumably, most of the smaller banks in the usa public markets are privately owned businesses, and presumably there is no usa Law that prevents a private bank from offering 100% reserve banking, limited services, and local loans if loaning money.

ANOTHER GOOD DAY WITH GOD

ANOTHER GOOD DAY WITH GOD

BUSINESS PLAN FOR: THE SIMPLE BANK, LCC

This bank will:

(1) "store" "legal tender" for the **10**
public.

(2) do bank-to-bank "legal tender"
transfers for the public, such as:
(a) transfer "legal tender" from a
bank in one state to a bank in
another state, and,
(b) transfer "legal tender" from a
bank in one country to a bank in
another country.

(3) "store" bank approved "general
tender" for the public.

(4) do bank-to-bank "general tender" transfers for the public, such as:

(a) transfer "general tender" from a bank in one state to a bank in another state, and,

(b) transfer "general tender" from a bank in one country to a bank in another country.

(5) facilitate a limited exchange of "legal tender" to/from some forms of "general tender" such as "legal tender" to/from "grain, shoes, silver, hemp seeds, and/or etc".

As an owner of a private bank, the banker could store any type of "General Tender", such as sacks of grain, shoes, silver, et cetera.

As a private bank, this bank may do bank-to-bank "money transfers" of grain, shoes, silver, "Legal Tender", et cetera, for a fee.

ANOTHER GOOD DAY WITH GOD

To save costs, this bank may be opened once a week, or once every two weeks, etc.

The bank may obtain minor revenue from withdraw and/or deposit fees, and money transfer fees for transferring "general tender" to and from various in-house banks and other participating banks.

As a simple bank, this bank will not offer an extensive list of banking services to the public, such as an extensive borrowing and lending service.

10

As a simple bank, the primary service of this bank will be to offer a "place of storage" of "legal tender" and/or "general tender".

ANOTHER GOOD DAY WITH GOD

It could be said that each "service" that was offered by a bank could singled-out and then be used as a reason to do a separate bank in and of itself;

for example, a bank that only offered one service to the public.

As far as regulating all the services offered by a bank, it can be presumed that many of the services offered has a set of laws and regulations that need to be complied with.

100's of services probably means 100's of laws and regulations, however, a bank owner that only offers one service to the public for example, probably does not need to deal with very many laws and regulations.

ANOTHER GOOD DAY WITH GOD

For example, a bank owner who only "stores" money for the public, probably only needs to comply with the same laws and regulations that any "household storage business" has to comply with;

For example, the public market could store their money at any "household storage business" just as easily as the public market could store their money at a "bank".

10

As a bank owner, you can offer the service of storing many more barter items, such as grain, shoes, silver, et cetera, that other banks do not offer as a service;

As a bank owner, you are not limited to storing the same items that other banks store;

ANOTHER GOOD DAY WITH GOD

Other banks may not offer the service of storing sacks of grain and silver, but your bank can offer the service; as a storage service, and not a borrowing and lending service, you will not have to deal with borrowing and lending the grain and silver, but the owner now has a means of storing their sacks of grain and silver, and perhaps a means of doing long distance money transfers using the various participating in-house banks that offer similar services as your bank.

Bartering with various items that are not "legal tender", is legal in the usa and many other countries, and therefore, perhaps your bank can offer the same storage services for many of those barter items.

Your bank can refrain from storing paper money and can refrain from doing money transfers with paper money.

ANOTHER GOOD DAY WITH GOD

Your bank can offer a storage and transfer service for various types of barter items that are not paper money, and thereby increase the habitual and common use of those barter items during common barter transactions in the public market.

10

ANOTHER GOOD DAY WITH GOD

ANOTHER GOOD DAY WITH GOD

====================================
BOYCOTTING GOLD   11
====================================

How did the ownership of gold go from many persons, who first obtained various tid-bits of gold, to the ownership of smaller groups of persons such as "governments", and others such as money changers doing their "central" bank scams ?

It seems that many of those little chunks of gold and little sparkles of gold that were gathered by the public from the natural public display in nature, seems to have been swindled from the public into the vaults of a minority group.

For example, it seems that swindlers in the usa "government" swindled gold from the public majority using a scheme called the "**bretton woods agreements act of 1962**", and then canceled the bretton woods agreement about 10 years later, and then, the swindlers swindled more gold using gold confiscation acts to pay for the overprinted paper money.

11

ANOTHER GOOD DAY WITH GOD

Was it constitutional for "president" nixon to suspend the Law, namely the "bretton woods agreement act of 1962" ?

Instead of enforcing the Law and preventing the overprinting of the paper money receipts for the gold, "president" nixon just "suspended" the bretton woods agreement and then heisted the gold ?

And now, several years after all that gold was heisted, there is some talk about using a "gold standard", that will presumably set the price of gold above its fair market value as compared to when gold was easier to locate.

ANOTHER GOOD DAY WITH GOD

"Raising" the price of gold, seems to benefit various minority groups that have done their confiscation schemes throughout history, such as:

* the gold heisted from russia from the bolshevik jews;

* the gold heisted again from the white russians in the gulag work camps;

*the gold heisted from various european crusades;

* the gold heisted from various european jewish bank paper money schemes;

* the gold heisted during the "suspension" of the "bretton woods agreements act";

* et cetera.

ANOTHER GOOD DAY WITH GOD

If the price of gold is set above
its fair market value when gold
was easier to locate, then that
will give the swindlers holding
the bulk of that swindled gold an
unfair increase in value of their
gold; as a result, more labor-time
would be required for the same
gram of gold ?

As said, many of the current bulk
holders of gold, are the same
swindlers who suspended the
bretton woods agreements act, and
the same swindlers who did various
other gold confiscation schemes in
the usa.

Using a "gold standard" set by the
usa "government" probably will
benefit the swindlers, and will
allow the swindlers to inflate the
price of their gold in the public
market.

May I suggest refusing to accept
gold at an inflated price, and
thereby causing the price of gold
held by the swindlers to be
reduced to the LESS THAN FAIR
market value of gold.

ANOTHER GOOD DAY WITH GOD

Without a Law, the public market can set the price of gold themselves, such as refusing to accept gold for more than the price of aluminum.

The only persons who put a price on gold is: (1) the "government" in a law, such as the "bretton woods agreements act of 1962", and, (2) the Public Market itself.

11

The only reason I am not suggesting boycotting gold completely, is because there are several industrial applications of gold, such as gold tinting, gold enamel, etc.

That said, if I refused to accept gold at a price more than the price of aluminum, then how much is gold worth ? (Gold would be the same price of aluminum.)

If the majority of the public market refuses to accept gold for a price more than the price of aluminum, then what does that do to the swindlers who swindled the bulk of gold throughout years ?

ANOTHER GOOD DAY WITH GOD

Perhaps the bretton woods agreements act, and the various gold confiscation acts, were all a swindle by the money changers to swindle gold from usa citizens and others.

For example, it can be argued that the bretton woods agreements act did not need to be suspended, and that instead of suspending the bretton woods agreement, the swindlers in the usa "government" could have enforced the printing of paper money, and suspended over-printing of the paper.

It can be argued that the persons demanding their payment of gold under the bretton woods agreement could have been offered other viable "items", such as silver and hemp seed.

Many persons often talk about "gold" as being a good "money", however, "gold" is perhaps not as good as other barter items, as discussed in this book.

ANOTHER GOOD DAY WITH GOD

```
====================================
BOYCOTTING PAPER MONEY          12
====================================
```

One of the main consistent
problems of pieces of paper being
used as "money" is that swindlers
tend to infiltrate governments and
over print paper money to be put
into their bank accounts;

Also, paper money tends to be
counterfeited by other swindlers
also;

12

There is a way to protect paper
money from being illegally
counterfeited, however, warmongers
in "governments" often tend to
pass "laws" that allow over
printing of paper money,
especially during a "war", or to
"protect" the "country";

Swindlers in "governments" also
tend to pass "laws" that allow
over printing paper money to be
given or lent to just about any
"country" or group who wants to
participate in a heist of paper
money.

ANOTHER GOOD DAY WITH GOD

Pieces of paper, when used as a TOKEN OF LABOR-TIME, often has been used as a representation for other tangible items that were deposited in a "bank", such as gold and silver, but paper in and of itself does not represent much labor-time to produce; if schemers and scammers can devise ways to get a majority of persons to use unpegged pieces of paper as money, and say that only they can produce the pieces of paper (of a certain size, printing, etc), then the schemers and scammers can swindle many persons ?

The history of paper money CAN NOT be older than the history of paper itself, and therefore, all the scams and swindles using paper money are not older than the history of paper.

ANOTHER GOOD DAY WITH GOD

In the usa "government", there are 3 branches of "government" that supposedly provide checks and balances to each other, but as a "democratic" "country", there is actually a forth branch of "government" called the "usa citizens".

Perhaps the fourth branch of usa "government" should boycott the use of all unpegged paper money in the Public Market (except perhaps to pay taxes to the other 3 branches of usa "government" according to law), and begin to do accept non-paper competing currencies during all private BARTER transactions, such as accepting metal, hemp oil, hemp seeds, bales of cotton, etc ?

Perhaps the fourth branch of usa "government" should force the other three branches of usa "government" to stop using paper money.

12

ANOTHER GOOD DAY WITH GOD

Not using paper money will be more cumbersome, and lazy citizens may prefer carrying paper money rather than carrying an item that is heavier such as a metal or a gallon of hemp oil, however, there are many benefits for boycotting paper money:

1. not using paper money will be a safeguard against counterfeiting/inflation from foreign and domestic swindlers in the usa "government" and elsewhere.

2. not using paper money will be a safeguard preventing swindlers in the usa "government" from having immediate paper money to pay for unnecessary extended wars; not using paper money hinders unnecessary wars; a "necessary" war probably does not even need "money".

3. not using paper money will be a safeguard preventing swindlers in the usa "government" from borrowing extensive amounts of unpegged paper "money" from a private central bank and from putting the usa into substantial usa debt, as is indicated at usdebtclock.org.

Is it more inconvenient to:
(a) occasionally carry around NON-PAPER money, such as a ball & chain, or,
(b) let warmongers in the usa "government" easily pay for an UNNECESSARY offensive war using pieces of paper that they overprint ?

12

Is it more inconvenient to:
(a) occasionally carry around NON-PAPER money, such as a ball & chain, or,
(b) do FREE SLAVE LABOR for the banker cabal and other foreign and domestic swindlers by means of accepting those counterfeit overprinted pieces of paper at the cash register in exchange for goods and services ?

ANOTHER GOOD DAY WITH GOD

In an adult-supervised uncorrupted utopia, modestly paid trustees could print and give paper money to anyone, as a TOKEN OF LABOR-TIME, whenever anyone did any type of approved labor;

There seems to be plenty of "work/tasks" available to do, but often the lack of funding stops the "work/tasks" from being done;

Even picking up a twig and putting the twig into a compost pile is "work", but often the lack of funding stops the "work/tasks" from being done;

In an utopia, there there could be a list of approved "jobs" available doing just about any type of work, such as any type of service work that did not produce a product, such as elevated roads, bridges, rubbish collection;

And after doing the work, the person could then get paid the appropriate amount of TOKENS OF LABOR-TIME directly by the trustee;

ANOTHER GOOD DAY WITH GOD

Other jobs could include paying
for any type of product or service
the "buyer" or "seller" to get a
free ride, such as paying paper
money to a dentist to give free
dental work to someone who was
capable of working for the paper
money himself.

Another example of paying for
products is where the trustees
always buys every product in the
Public Market and then puts the
products into a large "government"
store for resale; because real
labor was performed to produce
each of those products, the paper
money paid would later be accepted
in the Public Market, however, it
would more efficient to tell the
Public Market what needs to
produced most rather than letting
someone produce billions of
unneeded hammers.

12

ANOTHER GOOD DAY WITH GOD

In the adult-supervised
uncorrupted utopia, the TOKENS OF
LABOR-TIME would be accepted at
the cash register because the
"Seller" would be assured that the
paper TOKEN represents a TOKEN OF
LABOR-TIME for work that was
actually done, and would be
assured that trillions of dollars
of paper money is being lent to
someone at 0% interest where they
would be obtaining the paper money
without doing any actual work.

ANOTHER GOOD DAY WITH GOD

```
====================================
FUNDING NECESSARY WARS, VERSUS,
FUNDING UNNECESSARY WARS      13
====================================
```

As said, not using paper money
will be a safeguard to prevent
swindlers in the usa "government"
from having immediate access to
paper money funds to pay for
unnecessary extended wars;

If a "country" REALLY attacks
another "country" FOR REAL, then
it can be presumed that the
citizens would defend their
country FOR FREE without any
payment, if their "country" was
really being attacked.

13

ANOTHER GOOD DAY WITH GOD

However, instead of fighting for FREE, the citizens would probably demand to get paid to fight for those wars where the usa "government" wants to do unnecessary offensive wars of plunder, or during those wars that become more offensive rather than defensive;

And to pay the citizens, the usa "government" would need "money"; and without (unpegged) paper "money", the usa "government" would need to get tangible "money", such as hemp seeds, from the tax payers, and in that situation, if the tax payers did not want to fund the unnecessary offensive war, then the usa "government" would not be able to pay the "army" and the war would probably would stop from lack of funding.

ANOTHER GOOD DAY WITH GOD

In conclusion:

(1) the usa "government" needs money to pay a citizen army to fight as mercenaries in an unnecessary offensive war, and a country using paper money easily allows their usa "government" to easily and quickly pay for unnecessary offensive wars;

(2) a country that does not use paper money will be able to protest and perhaps stop the usa "government" from doing unnecessary offensive wars simply by not paying taxes to the usa "government";

13

(3) paper money is not necessary to pay citizens to defend their country, and citizens will defend their country from foreign attack for free if the country is genuinely under attack.

ANOTHER GOOD DAY WITH GOD

```
===================================
COMPETING CURRENCIES,
AND  "GOLD MONEY" VERSUS
"HEMP SEED MONEY"              14
===================================
```

Many persons in the past suggested
that "gold" is a good "money",
however, there may be better
BARTER items that can be used as
"money".

I want to first explain the
"value" of gold as follows...

14

ANOTHER GOOD DAY WITH GOD

(1) The hourglass value of gold has extreme fluctuations;

for example, someone could walk 7 feet and find a large two tonne chunk of gold;

whereas, someone else could spend a decade locating one tonne of little speckles of gold;

what is the value of the two tonne chunk of gold compared to the one tonne of gold ?

Using the hourglass standard, the two tonne chunk of gold has a value of about 2 hourglasses of time, and the one tonne of gold has a value of many thousands of hourglasses of time;

as a result, the value of two piles of gold is not equal when comparing the amounts of hourglass time needed to initially acquire gold from person to person;

(2) To acquire gold there may be additional costs to get certain authorizations to trespass and to get permits;

as a result, not very many persons will be able to acquire gold from the landscape, and will need to rely on acquiring what is already in the public market.

(3) Also, there may be environmental costs in acquiring gold from the landscape as the result of tearing up the billion year old natural landscape and tossing chemicals into the ground; **14**

removing gold from the landscape also irreversibly removes all the golden speckles that naturally adorn the landscape - perhaps most of the natural golden speckles are all now gone;

(4) revised "gold standards" in the public market can intentionally raise the price of gold above the real value of gold, in attempts to peg smaller and smaller amounts of scarce gold to a "dollar", and therefore, the persons holding the bulk of gold will "profit" from those raised prices of gold.

ANOTHER GOOD DAY WITH GOD

In comparison, some of the benefits and value of using hemp seed money as a competing currency are as follows...

(1) just about anyone in the public market needing "money" could grow some hemp to acquire some "hemp seed money";

(2) hemp seeds contain hemp seed oil; hemp seed oil can be used for hemp soap;

because many persons like using soap and presumably would be willing to store thousands of bars of soap, the hemp seed oil can be a viable form of money;

14

the value of hemp seed oil can therefore presumably could remain constant, if persons are willing to store thousands of bars of soap, or thousands of barrels of hemp seeds;

(3) the hemp seed oil that is in hemp seeds presumably will store for hundreds of years, and if humans cease to exist, there presumably will be a big piles of hemp seed and hemp seed oil sitting around;

(4) hemp seeds are also a form of edible protein, and many persons may also become accustomed to growing hemp seed for food;

(5) the hemp stalks are also used in industrial applications, such as clothes, rope, textiles, etc; hemp stalks are also another form of "money", just as bales of cotton are a form of "money";

(6) one benefit of the public market accepting "hemp seeds" during barter transactions is that just about any "jobless" person can grow some hemp for "hemp seed money"; in comparison, those "jobless" persons may be in a socially oppressive situation if forced to speculate for gold and obtain the necessary permits to obtain some gold "money";

(7) "hemp seed money" is "fair" in the amounts of hourglass time needed to initially acquire "hemp seeds" from person to person, and country to country.

In conclusion, items such as hemp seed "money" are better than gold "money"; just about anyone can procure hemp seed money in just about any country; one kilogram of hemp seeds in the usa, has the same value as one kilogram of hemp seeds in another country.

Using hemp seeds as money is just one example of using different BARTER items as money to lessen the need to use gold as money;

14

History shows that many of the BARTER items in the public market today, such as cotton, salt, iron, copper, silver, et cetera, were all used as "money" during barter transactions throughout history, and in actuality, those same BARTER items are still actually being used as "money" today in the public markets;

ANOTHER GOOD DAY WITH GOD

One difference between the stores in the public markets today versus the stores in the ancient public markets, is that the stores in the public markets today have reduced the forms of "accepted payment" during their BARTER transactions, and have narrowed their "accepted payments" to paper money;

There is not any law that prevents stores in the public markets today from accepting other forms of "barter payment" during during barter transactions in addition to accepting paper money.

The stores in the public markets today can accept hemp seed money, gold money, cotton money, grain money, salt money, et cetera.

The public market does not need the usa "government" to set a "gold standard"; the stores in the public market just need to start accepting those other barter items during their barter transactions.

ANOTHER GOOD DAY WITH GOD

Paper Money is recent in history, and many money changers and others swindlers seem to be alleging that one benefit of using paper money is that the money changers can easily increase or decrease the supply of money as necessary, and alleged that adjusting the supply of Paper Money is something that could not be done with a limited supply of other BARTER items, such as gold and silver.

However, "legal tender" does not have to be limited to just gold, silver, and paper money as discussed in a previous Chapter; history shows that ANY barter item can be used as "legal tender"; the public market could use "hemp seeds" as money; "hemp seed money" can easily be increased when various persons actually do some work by growing more "hemp seed money"; money CAN grow on trees;

15

ANOTHER GOOD DAY WITH GOD

The argument of "unlimited paper money" is perhaps false, because there could presumably be a paper shortage.

Some argue for a "gold standard", however, the hourglass value of gold fluctuates from gold pile to gold pile, and gold can be hoarded, and there does not seem to be an unlimited supply of shiny gold inside the billion year old landscape, and therefore, there may be occasions where there is a significant gold shortage in the public market if gold is used as the ONLY "legal tender".

Because of the scarcity of gold, perhaps it would be better to use several BARTER items as "legal tender", and as "common tender", such as "hemp seeds".

Generally speaking, just about any BARTER item that is often used in industry and that can be produced by just about anyone in the public market, would be a good "legal tender";

ANOTHER GOOD DAY WITH GOD

It has been suggested that "clay bricks" can be used as "money";

The public market does not need to wait for the usa "government" to "allow" the public market to use "hemp seed" or "clay bricks" as "money" in the public market in BARTER transactions that does not Legally require the use of "Legal Tender";

The buyers and sellers in the Public Market are the only persons hindering the acceptance of competing currencies at the cash register, not the usa "government" or the "central banks".

15

One argument against using one or two BARTER items as money seems to be that the "money" can be "hoarded", however, hoarding probably should be encouraged just as a chipmunk "hoards" nuts;

113

Instead of just accepting one or two BARTER items as "money", if the public market begins accepting many different items as "money", then "hoarding" of any particular BARTER item should not be an issue;

Also, to promote the use of many different BARTER items as "money", the usa "government" simply needs to declare that certain items are free from sales tax during BARTER transactions;

For example, when a paper dollar is BARTERED for another BARTER item, the paper dollar does not receive a sales tax, but the second BARTER item does receive a sales tax;

If the sales tax was removed from the second BARTER item, then the second BARTER item would also be encouraged to be used as "money" in the Public Market;

ANOTHER GOOD DAY WITH GOD

====================================
ARE FEDERAL TAXES IN THE USA A
FARCE ?   **16**
====================================

Aside from the usa dollar being
called the petro-dollar, after all
the paper money in the usa was
unpegged from gold or other
commodity in the 1970's when the
"bretton woods agreements act of
1962" was (unconstitutionally?)
suspended, then why does the usa
"government" need to "borrow"
those unpegged pieces of paper
(at interest) from the privately
owned jewish central bank called
the "federal reserve" ?

16

If the usa paper money is unpegged
from any commodity, and if the
unpegged paper money has the value
of a piece of paper, and if the
usa "government" could just print
the unpegged paper money
themselves, then why does the usa
"government" need to do a public
song and dance for the citizens
about needing to collect "taxes"
from the citizens ?

ANOTHER GOOD DAY WITH GOD

Perhaps the only reason that the usa "government" does a song and dance about needing pieces of paper money from the citizens, is because many persons in the usa "government" have been told that they need to collect "taxes", and are in the HABIT of collecting "taxes", and no one seems to have really noticed that those same pieces of paper are now completely unpegged from the bretton woods gold, and that each of those pieces of paper have the actual value of paper;

Aside from the usa "government" doing a petro-dollar agreement with foreign countries, that gives usa military weapons to a foreign country in exchange for usa pieces of paper and their agreement to sell oil only for those usa pieces of paper, all usa paper money is not necessarily pegged to any commodity;

ANOTHER GOOD DAY WITH GOD

Even with the (unconstitutional?) petro-dollar agreement, the usa "government" is not restricted from printing the pieces of paper themselves.

What if the usa "government" said that instead of collecting "taxes", that they were going to borrow the unpegged paper money from the jewish central bank, and then pay the jewish central bank "interest" on the borrowed unpegged paper money, and then print the unpegged paper money themselves to pay the "interest" to the jewish central bank for getting the "loan" of paper.

16

Or better, instead of the deceptive song and dance, what if the usa "government" said they were going to abolish the FEDERAL RESERVE ACT, stop collecting taxes from the citizens, and then just print all the unpegged paper money themselves to get their "taxes" ?

ANOTHER GOOD DAY WITH GOD

Perhaps one reason that the jewish central bank is able to continue their bank charter under the FEDERAL RESERVE ACT to do their "lending" of the pieces of paper to the usa "government", is because the jewish bankers in the jewish central bank are able to thwart any member of the usa "congress" who begins to suggest repealing the FEDERAL RESERVE ACT to give the exclusive right to the usa "government" to print their own paper money ?

ANOTHER GOOD DAY WITH GOD

```
====================================
IS THE USA "GOVERNMENT" BORROWING
PAPER MONEY A FARCE ?            17
====================================
```

Is it a farce that the usa "government" borrows UNPEGGED paper money from a privately owned jewish central bank called the federal reserve ?

The usdebtclock.org indicates that the usa debt is about 20 trillion dollars.

Did the usa "government" borrow most of the 20 trillion dollars from the privately owned jewish central bank ?

17

Where did the jewish central bank get 20 trillion dollars ?

If the jewish central bank was forced to peg all the paper money "lent" to a commodity, then it can be presumed that the jewish central bank would have significantly less than 20 trillion dollars to lend.

ANOTHER GOOD DAY WITH GOD

Is the so-called "debt" from the "borrowed" unpegged paper money a jewish money changer scam ?

Perhaps the jewish central bank would not even be concerned about "lending" 100 trillion pieces of unpegged paper money to the usa "government", because the jewish money changers have devised a paper money scheme as recent as the history of paper itself, to get all their gentile "slaves" to use the paper money in the Public Market, and thereby getting the Public Market to accept that portion of the paper money that the jews got for free as "interest" from lending the unpegged paper money to the usa "government";

What would happen if a majority of the usa citizens forced the usa "congress" to Repeal the "federal reserve act of 1913", and to print an non-redeemable 20 trillion dollar paper dollar to "repay" the jewish central bank ?

ANOTHER GOOD DAY WITH GOD

If various money changers have
been doing a "central" bank scam
for the previous 300 years doing
their unpegged paper money scam,
then what are those money changers
going to do if the public market
begins refusing to use paper money
for "goods and services".

What are those swindler money
changers going to do if they are
forced to do a rush-riot money
exchange to convert their hoard of
paper money to "items" with
substantial "hourglass value" ?

Obviously, many swindler jewish   **18**
money changers, such as the
rothschild's, warburg's, and
others, are going to loose most of
their "trillions" of easily
swindled paper dollars they
acquired during their 300 year
paper money scam.

ANOTHER GOOD DAY WITH GOD

Any shop owner who is financially in a situation to determine what the shop owner will accept as payment, can begin sooner than later to refuse unpegged paper money as payment, whereas, many shop owners more desperate for "money" may need to continue accepting paper "money" until more and more barter is done without unpegged paper money.

ANOTHER GOOD DAY WITH GOD

HOW ARE TAXES PAID IN A PUBLIC
MARKET THAT DOES "DIRECT BARTER
TRADING" ?   **19**

How is taxation possible if the
public market uses more direct
barter trades ?

Fortunately for tax payers, the
usa "government" still issues
"silver coins" as "Legal Tender",
and therefore, the public market
can acquire just enough silver
coins to pay their taxes;

For example, from the 100% of
wages that are paid to employees,
a percentage such as 5% is used to
pay an income tax, and that 5%
could be paid to the employee as
"silver coins";   **19**

For example, an employee can be
paid their first or last yearly
paycheck using "silver coins", so
the employee can pay income tax at
the end of the year, and then the
employee can be paid other "items"
throughout the year as wages.

ANOTHER GOOD DAY WITH GOD

For example, a grocery store can accept "General Tender" from customers, but allow customers and others to barter using their surplus "silver coins" to enable the grocery store to pay taxes.

Buyers and sellers during barter transactions can always ask if the buyer and seller already has enough silver coins to pay taxes when determining what types of "items" to use during the barter transaction.

Another issue with direct barter trading, is how the "goods and services" are going to be "taxed" by the usa "government" ?

For example, if the "sales tax" is 5%, is a seller of shoes and a seller of grain who does a direct trade barter transaction each the buyer or each the seller ?

If the sales tax is %%, does each buyer pay a 5% sales tax, for a combined total of a 10% sales tax ?

ANOTHER GOOD DAY WITH GOD

And how is the usa "government" going to determine the values of those "items" traded during the direct trade barter transaction, for tax purposes ?

Until the usa public controls the usa "government", it can be presumed that the freeloading usa "government" is going to continue wanting alot of free "money" from the public, and will therefore get involved in the whole BARTER transaction scene to determine how much free "money" the usa "government" is going to be paid.

19

ANOTHER GOOD DAY WITH GOD

ANOTHER GOOD DAY WITH GOD

```
====================================
IS THE NEED FOR BARTER AND MONEY
OVER EMPHASIZED IN SOCIETY ?    20
====================================
```

It has been said that the theory
of money presupposes the theory of
the saleableness of goods.

Although, perhaps both money and
domestic/international bartering
are over rated.

A society with members that are
each approximately 100% self-
sufficient would not need to
barter very much, and would not
need very much "money" for
bartering - to the detriment of
parasitic jewish swindlers and
other swindlers in the usa
"government" and banks.

How is the usa "government", or   **20**
any government, going to collect
"taxes", or receive free "goods
and services", from a society with
members that are each
approximately 100% self-sufficient
?

ANOTHER GOOD DAY WITH GOD

Until the usa public controls the usa "government", it can be presumed that many persons in the usa "government" are going to want to continue getting free "goods and services" from the public, and will therefore get involved in the whole self-sufficient no-barter scene to determine how they are going to get their free ride.

How are the jewish swindlers going to continue paying "slaves" with their unpegged bogus paper money scam, if their so-called "cattle/slaves" are the residents of a village that is approximately 100% self-sufficient and is not trying to sell any "goods and services" to those jewish swindlers and other outsiders ?

ANOTHER GOOD DAY WITH GOD

One alternative to one person being completely self-sufficient and refusing to "sell" any products, is for the person to be in a larger group, such as a self-sufficient village, and then, the village could do "money background checks" of visitors to **avoid being a "cattle/slave" to any jewish swindler who is bringing a sack of overprinted unpegged paper money that they got for 0% interest from some jewish bank.**

Also, if many villages are self-sufficient, then those self-sufficient villages obviously would decrease domestic and international bartering, however, perhaps domestic and international bartering is over-rated.

For example, perhaps a more cost efficient model for international bartering would limit international barter transactions to bulk raw materials that are needed for domestic use in the domestic public markets, and to exceptionally better quality goods.

20

For example, international bartering involves shipping and handling, and therefore, shipping and handling will naturally increase the costs of goods, and therefore, the price of those imported goods may need to be decreased to compete with the domestic goods of similar quality, and as a result, the workers who fashioned those goods are earning less for their time and labor.

If the international public markets limited their bartering to bulk raw materials and, exceptionally better quality goods, then by keeping a majority of their domestically produced goods in their domestic public markets, the shipping and handling costs can be reduced throughout the international public markets, and the domestic workers will get a larger storehouse for their own domestic labor.

ANOTHER GOOD DAY WITH GOD

If a person has a pair of shoes valued at two hourglasses, and another person has a sack of grain valued at 2 hourglasses, and then the two sellers do a barter transaction, then there does not seem to be any "profit" involved.

However, if the seller of shoes wants a "profit" and raises the price of a pair of shoes from 2 hourglasses to 3 hourglasses, and the seller of grain also wants a "profit" and raises the price of a sack of grain from 2 hourglasses to 3 hourglasses, and then the two persons do a barter transaction, then who earned a "profit" ?

However during each barter transaction, each seller had to pay a 10% sales tax, and therefore, when the sales price was increased, each seller had to pay more taxes while still did not earning a "profit"; as a result, who really "profited" ?

21

ANOTHER GOOD DAY WITH GOD

And if the person selling shoes was the only person who raised the price of shoes from 2 hourglasses to 3 hourglasses, forcing the other person to barter a sack of grain valued at 3 hourglasses for the shoes valued at 2 hourglasses, then is that a fair barter transaction ? Who is the "slave" doing an hourglass of free labor ?

Without Laws setting the "sale price" of "goods and services", such as setting the prices using the fair hourglass standard, various buyers and sellers in the public market will greedily raise the prices of their goods and services as they each try to swindle other members of the public market for extra hourglasses than what is actually worked for - this could be called "The theory of greed in a public market without fixed sales prices".

Of course it probably would be fair to raise the hourglass price to pay for transportation and storage fees.

ANOTHER GOOD DAY WITH GOD

A slave is a person who does labor for another person for free.

What is the difference between a slave and a "free" tax payer ? A slave is taxed 100%, minus room and board.

It can be said that over-taxation beyond what is actually required to pay for the "services" of the usa "government" is a form of slavery, where alot of extra free money is going to freeloaders in the usa "government".

If a person pays 25% tax a year in the usa for sales-tax and for state/federal income-tax, then that person is working 25% of the year for free; a 25% yearly tax is equivalent to 3 months labor in a year.

22

ANOTHER GOOD DAY WITH GOD

Are the state/federal employees in the usa doing very much work for your money, or are those employees trying to get a free ride by over-taxing their slaves ?

Overprinted and Counterfeited paper money is also a form of slavery, because the counterfeiters get free money without working for the money, and then the counterfeiters "pay" their "slaves" with the counterfeited paper money in exchange for "goods and services";

The counterfeiters can also be in a foreign or domestic "central bank", because one way for counterfeiters to legally do international slavery is to use their privately owned "central banks" to overlend unpegged paper money at interest, and to also lend the unpegged paper money to themselves at 0% interest, such as is allegedly being done by the international jewish rothschilds central bank scheme.

ANOTHER GOOD DAY WITH GOD

Many persons complain about the "banks".

Banks can be boycotted.

The advantage of using the Simple Bank as described above is that money is not lent to the public, and therefore,

any financial swindles done by banks that lend money using fractional reserves may not effect those persons who just "stored" their money in the vault of the Simple Bank;

Those persons who deposit their money at the Simple Bank, especially if the deposits are deposits of "General Tender", may not be effected by any financial swindles done by the banks that lend money, and may not be effected by any financial swindles done by the usa "government".

23

ANOTHER GOOD DAY WITH GOD

No one is forcing anyone to borrow money from a bank, or to put a mortgage on their property;

Perhaps it would be better to avoid borrowing any money from the lending banks ?

ANOTHER GOOD DAY WITH GOD

```
===================================
WHO HAS A TRILLION DOLLARS ?    24
===================================
```

If all the "money" in existence
consisted of tangible items, could
there be a trillionaire ?

Can anyone be a trillionaire
without fiat money ?

Is there really trillions of
"dollars" in existence ?

Was real labor performed to
acquire the trillions of "dollars"
?

If real products and services were
traded for the trillions of
dollars, then what were the
products and services ?

24

ANOTHER GOOD DAY WITH GOD

For example, usdebtclock.org indicates that the usa has about 20 trillion dollars debt; the usa "government" borrows money from the privately owned federal reserve central bank set up with the federal reserve act of 1913 that was lobbied by the jewish bankers;

If the federal reserve was required to do 100% reserve lending, then the privately owned federal reserve central bank probably would not have been able to lend 20 trillion dollars ?

Presumably, most of the pieces of paper in existence called "money" were printed and lent with 0% reserves in the banks, and therefore, just because a privately owned jewish central bank lends 1 trillion pieces of paper to someone, does not necessarily mean that the person is a real trillionaire; most of the trillions of paper dollars in existence are just pieces of paper (wood paper and electronic paper).

ANOTHER GOOD DAY WITH GOD

It is real easy for a "government" and "bankers" to counterfeit paper money using various schemes and then to say that trillions of dollars are being passed around, but what were the products and services that caused the trillions of dollars to be put into the economy ?

Also, pertaining to the question is there really trillions of "dollars" in existence, various "banks" in the Public Market are doing "fractional reserve lending", involving re-lending the unpegged paper storage receipts that are stored in the "bank" vault;

As a result, there appears to be alot of talk of "trillions" of dollars being owned and spent in the Public Market, but in reality, there probably is substantially less "money" in existence;

24

ANOTHER GOOD DAY WITH GOD

Soon after the Public Market once again begins (voluntarily) using tangible items as "money", it will become more apparent how much "money" is really in existence.

After the Public Market begins (voluntarily) using tangible items as "money", it may be like the game of musical chairs where some persons will be stuck with all those unpegged paper storage receipts, because many Buyers and Sellers in the Public Market will not accept the unpegged paper storage receipts.

For example, when Buyers and Sellers in the Public Market on begin doing BARTER trades only using goods that have substantial value, such as BARTERING silver for wheat, and BARTERING wheat for hemp seed, and BARTERING hemp seed for tables and chairs, then that will force all those persons who allegedly own "trillions" of unpegged paper storage receipts and bank account numbers, to bring to the Public Market only items with that substantial value;

ANOTHER GOOD DAY WITH GOD

A Buyer or Seller in the Public Market could refuse to accept a pile of unpegged paper storage receipts, and instead demand a pile of silver or hemp seed; that will force the persons who allegedly own "trillions" of unpegged paper storage receipts to validate their unpegged paper storage receipts for items with substantial value;

That said, it may be impossible to exchange a trillion unpegged paper storage receipts for an equivalent amount of items with substantial value;

In reality, a person who claims to own a "trillion dollars" does not actually own a "trillion dollars" if forced to exchange those unpegged paper storage receipts and unpegged bank numbers for items such a silver, wheat, hemp seed, tables and chairs;

24

ANOTHER GOOD DAY WITH GOD

Many of the persons who claim to own a "trillion dollars" may say that they own a bunch of gold worth a "trillion dollars", but the Public Market can also refuse to accept any gold at INFLATED prices;

One of the reasons gold has become used as "money" is because it requires time/labor to acquire, is somewhat scarce, and has a good shelf-life, but just because someone says gold is worth a "trillion dollars" does not mean the gold is worth a "trillion dollars";

Other items with substantial value also have similar qualifications to gold, therefore, the demand for gold at INFLATED prices may be low because there are other items that can also be used effective as "money" during a BARTER transaction.

ANOTHER GOOD DAY WITH GOD

After the Public Market once again begins using tangible items as "money", it will force people to quickly BARTER as much of the bogus unpegged paper storage receipts as possible in exchange for valid commodities, and then, it will really put to the test the notion of there being "trillions" of dollars in existence from what remains and how much tangible items each person actually has.

24

ANOTHER GOOD DAY WITH GOD

```
===================================
```
AMEND FEDERAL RESERVE ACT OF
1913 ?   **25**
```
===================================
```

There is some talk of abolishing the "federal reserve act of 1913", and thereby abolishing the privately owned jewish federal reserve central bank in the usa, and perhaps that would be good for the domestic and foreign economy.

A possible alternative to completely abolishing the "federal reserve act of 1913", would be to amend the federal reserve act saying that the privately owned federal reserve central bank must have 100% reserves for all paper money that the federal reserve lends, and/or that when lending money, the federal reserve must only lend tangible commodities, such as hemp seed and silver, and because of past swindles involving gold, all the gold lent by the federal reserve must not be lent at a price that is more than the price of aluminum by volume.

25

ANOTHER GOOD DAY WITH GOD

After such an amendment, the jewish bankers may voluntarily close the federal reserve because of an inability to do their paper money scam involving bogus paper money.

Who owns the stock in the privately owned central bank of the usa ?

Many jews collaborated to form the "federal reserve act of 1913", and it can be presumed that those same jews gave themselves the stock in the "privately owned central bank".

Since the owners of the usa central bank are not disclosed to the usa, including the usa "government", just about anyone could be owners of the federal reserve, such as england, iran, north korea, etc.

Why does the incompetent usa "government" allow a foreign central bank to operate in the usa ?

ANOTHER GOOD DAY WITH GOD

WAS THE SUSPENSION OF THE BRETTON
WOODS AGREEMENTS ACT OF 1962
CONSTITUTIONALLY LEGAL ?   **26**

Who gave richard nixon the
executive power to suspend the
congressionally enacted "bretton
woods agreements act of 1962" ?

Perhaps the "bretton woods
agreement act" should be
unsuspended ?

Did richard nixon have the
executive power to enforce the law
and prevent the paper money that
represented the gold that was
stored by the usa "government"
from being overprinted ?

As a result of richard nixon and
his croney's suspending the
"bretton woods agreement act", all
the usa paper storage receipts
were completely unpegged from all
the gold that was stored in the
usa vault and from any other
commodity;

26

ANOTHER GOOD DAY WITH GOD

In effect, certain persons in the usa "government" heisted all the gold for themselves.

In effect, all the gold in the usa vault was stolen and transferred from a majority of persons to a minority group of bank heister's.

So that is how all that gold in the usa vault was transferred from the majority to a smaller minority group of "governments".

Surely a majority of the persons who deposited their gold into the usa gold vault did not overprint bogus paper storage receipts, but instead of enforcing the counterfeit laws and stopping the overprinting, richard nixon suspended the "bretton woods agreements act", allowed the overprinting of bogus paper money, and kept the gold;

ANOTHER GOOD DAY WITH GOD

The minority group of persons in the usa "government" punished the majority instead of punishing themselves and the privately owned jewish federal reserve central bank.

After the paper storage receipts were unpegged from the gold, someone in the usa "government" connived a different scam called the "petro-dollar"; the "petro-dollar" scam probably is not an official usa law, but probably is an unofficial agreement with certain "countries" that sell oil, that they must raise the price of their oil, and then only sell their oil to other "countries" in exchange for the unpegged usa paper storage receipts; in exchange for participating in the "petro-dollar" scam, the usa "government" agreed to sell military weapons and other goods and services to those "countries" who are selling the oil.

26

ANOTHER GOOD DAY WITH GOD

As a result of the "petro-dollar" scam, the privately owned jewish federal reserve central bank could continue over-lending the unpegged usa paper storage receipts; this over-lending of paper money apparently has continued, because many of the "countries" wanting to buy the oil first needed to get the unpegged paper storage receipts to buy the oil.

As a result of the "petro-dollar" scam and the continued demand for the unpegged paper storage receipts, many persons did not seem to really notice an effect that the paper storage receipts were unpegged from gold, and that those paper storage receipts are actually suppose to be pegged to something to have a value consistent with the denomination printed on the paper storage receipts.

ANOTHER GOOD DAY WITH GOD

As a result of the usa "government" now needing to "borrow" UNPEGGED paper storage receipts from the jewish central bank AT INTEREST (ha ha ha ha ha ha ha), according to the "federal reserve act of 1913", it can be presumed that vast quantities of bogus paper storage receipts were borrowed, spent, and lent by the privately owned jewish central bank and their croney's in the usa "government";

An example of privately owned jewish central bank over-lending bogus paper money is at usdebtclock.org; according to usdebtclock.org, the usa debt is now about 20 trillion dollars;

How much of those trillions of UNPEGGED paper storage receipts "lent" to the usa "government" AT INTEREST from the jewish central bank actually represent a commodity stored in a vault ?

26

ANOTHER GOOD DAY WITH GOD

For those unfamiliar with paper being pegged to gold, during recent history, pieces of paper were given to persons after depositing their gold for storage at the "bank", as a receipt that could be redeemed at any time during business hours for the gold.

Eventually, the paper storage receipts themselves were traded directly in the public market without anyone withdrawing the gold first;

This trading of the paper receipts was able to be done because the paper storage receipts could be redeemed by anyone, and always represented the actual gold that was stored in the vaults.

Soon the gold smiths that were operating various "banks" in the Public Market began lending extra (counterfeit) paper storage receipts that did not necessarily represent any gold stored in the vaults;

ANOTHER GOOD DAY WITH GOD

This scam of lending bogus paper receipts apparently is a scam that many khazarian fake jews and their croney's really fight to "legalize" throughout the recent history of paper.

For example, the usa began storing gold in exchange for paper storage receipts according to the terms of the "bretton woods agreements act of 1962".

Once again, the money changers began doing the "banker" scheme of lending excessive bogus paper storage receipts (called the usa paper dollar), presumably in violation of the terms the "bretton woods agreements act of 1962";

Eventually, if it was not already a part of the long-term "banker" scam, many "countries" began suspecting that the paper money receipts were being over printed, and then tried redeeming a bulk of their paper storage receipts for the gold stored in the vaults;

26

ANOTHER GOOD DAY WITH GOD

When "countries" tried redeeming their paper storage receipts, the usa president at the time, richard nixon, believed that instead of enforcing the terms of the "bretton woods agreements act of 1962" and preventing the over-lending of the bogus paper storage receipts, that it was better to suspend the "bretton woods agreements act" and heist all the gold from the majority.

ANOTHER GOOD DAY WITH GOD

(1) Try to bring happiness to GOD, the Creator of the Universe.

(2) It is painless to Help end human suffering by not reproducing;

Telling everyone that they can avoid reproducing to painlessly help end human suffering probably has never been done.

(3) A substitute to eating animal protein is eating:
(a) beans and rice, and vitamin b12, and
(b) soybeans and vitamin b12, and
(c) hemp seed and vitamin b12.